# A STRANGE SERVANT

# A Strange Servant

## A RUSSIAN FOLKTALE

**illustrated by**
**PAUL GALDONE**

**TRANSLATED BY BLANCHE ROSS**

ALFRED A. KNOPF  NEW YORK

THIS IS A BORZOI BOOK PUBLISHED BY ALFRED A. KNOPF, INC. Illustrations Copyright © 1977 by Paul Galdone. Text Copyright © 1977 by Alfred A. Knopf, Inc. All rights reserved under International and Pan-American Copyright Conventions. Published in the United States by Alfred A. Knopf, Inc., New York, and simultaneously in Canada by Random House of Canada Limited, Toronto. Distributed by Random House, Inc., New York. Manufactured in the United States of America. LIBRARY OF CONGRESS CATALOGING IN PUBLICATION DATA. Galdone, Paul. A strange servant. SUMMARY: A traditional Russian tale in which a wily beggar cleverly outwits three rich merchants by convincing them that his rabbit is really a magical servant. [1. Folklore—Russia] I. Title. PZ8.1.G15St [398.2] [E] 77-4563 ISBN 0-394-83453-4 ISBN 0-394-93453-9 lib. bdg.

*To Kathleen*

**N**ASSIR-YEDDIN had spent his whole life in poverty. But one day he found himself so poor that he had not a penny left to buy either a piece of bread to eat or a log to warm his house.

"What are we going to do?" asked his wife, weeping.

"Don't cry," he told her. "Though the days follow one another, they do not resemble each other. Today we no longer have anything, but tomorrow, if you do as I ask, we shall be provided for.

"Go to the butcher and, for the last time, get a piece of mutton on credit. Borrow from our neighbors some wood, flour and coffee. Promise them that you will return twice the amount by tomorrow. Then prepare a fine dinner to serve to the three noble guests I will bring home this evening."

"What foolishness are you hatching?" the wife protested. "This is no time to invite guests."

"You wait and see! But when we arrive at the house and you welcome us, be sure to exclaim: 'How late you are! It is a long time since our servant came to order the meal. Everything is ready—the roast, the pies, the cakes and the coffee.'"

"Our servant?" she asked, almost choking. "Where in the world have you fished one up?"

"I am going to get him now," he replied.

Dumbfounded, the unhappy woman told herself that her husband must have lost his mind.

Meanwhile Nassir-Yeddin went to one of his friends, a hunter, and asked him to let him have two rabbits which he had trapped the night before.

When he returned home, he told his wife: "Look, these are our servants. Let's lock up one in the pantry, and the other I'll take with me. You call Veliocha, the son of our neighbor,

and tell him to come and bring his violin. Have him go in the pantry, too. The minute Veliocha hears us enter the house, let him gaily tackle a tune of his choice. But when he hears our steps approaching the pantry, he must stop playing and hide. Be sure to carry out all my instructions to the letter."

"I shall obey you," said his wife. "You are never wrong."

Nassir-Yeddin took off with one of the rabbits tucked under his arm. He entered a noisy coffeehouse full of customers who were sitting about on rugs busily chatting and smoking their long pipes. He took a place near the entrance and began caressing the frightened rabbit.

Soon the people, surprised at what he was doing, began to tease him: "Is this your new method of hunting? How in heaven did you manage to catch this game?"

"It has nothing to do with hunting," he replied. "I have hired this rabbit."

"You *hired* him?"

"I did, and there is no magic to it. Just hiring a servant for a job. And really, I couldn't have found a more willing servant. All I have to do is utter my command, and immediately it is carried out. Who could rival such a valet?"

Amazed, the people thought he must be joking. "What a lot of nonsense!" they shouted in unison.

"But I'm not lying. I shall prove to you this instant that I'm telling the truth."

There were three rich merchants in the room, and he asked them to be his witnesses and given a decision in this matter.

"What do you want us to do?" they asked.

"Nothing extraordinary. Simply grant me the favor of visiting my home. I'm sending my servant with a message to my wife so that she can prepare a good dinner in your honor."

The three men, stung by curiosity, accepted the invitation at once.

"Let your wife know we shall gladly take some coffee."

"What?" he exclaimed, cunningly. "And have you leave my home famished? No, no, I want to treat you right."

Then he spoke very distinctly into the rabbit's ear: "You have heard, my friend, what our guests' wishes are. Go tell your mistress to make us coffee. But that is not enough. Ask her to roast a big leg of lamb and make some pies and some cakes."

Everyone smiled at this utter nonsense.

Having spoken thus, Nassir-Yeddin opened the door with a flourish. In one fast bound the rabbit disappeared around the street corner.

"You're not going to see that one in a hurry," the people said, scoffingly.

Then he sat down next to his guests. They chatted, smoked and sipped their coffee, until finally they left to go and have their dinner.

Nassir-Yeddin's wife looked a bit annoyed as she greeted them, according to her husband's instructions.

"You have taken your sweet time getting here. The dinner has been ready for ages," she said.

To their surprise, the guests saw the table covered with dishes of marvelous food.

"Who told you to expect three guests for dinner?"

"Our servant. It is quite a while since he brought my husband's message. If only he had told me that you would be late, too!"

The guests were flabbergasted, but they did not need to be coaxed to do the dinner justice.

"Really, he didn't forget a single thing!" they exclaimed, full of admiration. "Everything is here. The roast lamb, the pies, the cakes and the coffee."

The richest of the three, after having eaten and drunk his fill, asked, "And where is that paragon of a servant?"

"He is tired," replied Nassir-Yeddin, "and is resting in the pantry. Listen, and you will hear him playing the violin."

They bent their ears to listen and could actually hear some-one playing.

"I have never seen such a rabbit. Quick, show us this marvel!" pleaded the wealthy merchant. "I am always fasci-nated by strange and mysterious things that surpass under-standing."

The other two guests also pressed Nassir to show them this marvel.

"I'll be glad to show you my servant," he said, giving in at last to their pleas. "But you must stop your chattering and walk on tiptoe, because at the least noise he drops his bow and stops playing. A rabbit, as you know, is easily frightened. He will panic in front of strangers. And if he stops playing, all my pleading will be to no avail."

"We shall walk very quietly, without whispering even a single word. That's a promise," they said in unison.

"So be it. Let us go," their host replied.

Holding their carpet slippers in their hands, with their fingers pressed to their lips lest a sound escape, the notables followed Nassir-Yeddin to the back of the kitchen.

But upon hearing the music so close, the richest of the three was unable to contain his delight.

"Splendid, splendid!" he shouted ecstatically.

The violin-playing ceased at once.

"Why did you shout?" asked the master of the house disapprovingly. "Now my rabbit is frightened and will not play another note."

But the rich merchant, as if possessed, went on repeating: "Splendid, splendid, indeed!"

And his companions, bursting with admiration, joined him, exclaiming: "How wonderful! How wonderful! Quick, let us see this genius of an animal!"

Nassir, opening the door halfway, let the guests have a peak into the pantry. There they saw a violin lying on the floor and a terrified rabbit cringing in the farthest corner.

Nassir picked up the rabbit, fondled him gently, and said to him in a soothing voice, "Don't be scared, my little bunny. Come, keep on playing for our guests." But the fearful animal, trembling in all his limbs, just laid back his ears.

The richest of the merchants proposed right then and there to buy this extraordinary creature.

"Sell him to me," said the second merchant. "You'll make a better bargain!"

"Me, I don't haggle about the price!" said the third. "I'll give you whatever you ask for him."

"What! And let him escape right under my nose? Never!" shouted the first man, stamping his foot. "I was the one who spoke first."

Soon enough the whole house was ringing with the uproar.

Finally, Nassir-Yeddin broke in, saying calmly, "But I wouldn't think of giving up such a model servant who plays the violin so well. Besides, my wife is used to him and couldn't do without him. No, no, do not insist. I will not sell him."

Pleased as could be with how everything was going, the penniless man let the rich merchants go on baiting him, each one trying to outdo the others.

"I'll give you my embroidered tunic!"

"Me, I'll give you a mule. No—two, three mules!"

"I'll do better! I'll give you a hundred pieces of gold!"

They went on outbidding each other. But Nassir remained unmoved. Then at last his wife took a hand in the matter.

"It is an insult to Allah and an offense against hospitality to refuse anything to guests," she said.

Nassir heaved a sigh and said, "You are right!" Then, turning to the one who had made the highest offer, he said, "Give me your gold, but do it quickly before I change my mind."

The merchant hastened to seal the bargain. Then he pressed his hand to his heart and said to his friends, "Don't hold it against me. Allah willed it thus."

The others agreed that apparently it was the will of Allah, and they made up with him.

"And now," said the winner, "let us celebrate this happy event together."

"It is I who will give the orders," he told the rabbit. "Run to your new mistress and announce our arrival. Tell her to prepare another luxurious supper, to be ready later this evening after prayers, when I shall bring guests to the house. Go! Scram! Do not dawdle on your way, or she will stew you!"

He put him on the ground, and immediately the rabbit took off like a whirlwind.

Nassir and the merchants then whiled away the time in pleasant talk until it was time to go to the mosque.

After prayers they were about to set out for the supper when Nassir-Yeddin began to moan and groan: "Oh, my kidneys! Oh, my legs! I can't take another step. Forgive me. I think it is better if I go home."

It was very late when the three friends arrived at the luxurious home. Despite their loud and repeated knocks, no one answered the door.

At last, the merchant's wife dragged herself out of bed and opened the door for them. Yawning sleepily, she muttered, "What a time to bring home unexpected guests."

"What are you talking about? Didn't you expect us for supper?"

"Nobody told me to expect guests," she replied.

"Didn't my rabbit inform you of our coming?" asked the perplexed husband.

"What rabbit are you talking about? Have you lost your mind?"

"I'm talking about the rabbit, our new servant."

This was too much. She let her full rage burst forth. "Are you mocking me or have you gone crazy?" she shouted. And with that she slammed the door in their faces and went back to bed.

"That rogue has cheated me!" the merchant screamed, taking off like a hurricane for the poor peasant's house.

When he got there, he began shaking his fist at Nassir-Yeddin and yelling, "Traitor! Liar! Thief!"

But Nassir-Yeddin, lying on his couch, replied calmly, "Just in what way did I cheat you? I am not a liar. It is you who have deceived yourself."

"I? What are you talking about?" roared the outraged merchant.

"When you sent the rabbit to your home, did you tell him where you lived? On which street and in which house? I am not to blame."

The rich man slapped himself on the forehead. "That is true. I forgot to tell him."

"And what's more," said Nassir, "you didn't handle him properly. To threaten him with being stewed! He doesn't like such treatment. You have lost the best of servants, through your own fault. After all, you had to deal with a rabbit, not a dog."

The rich fool just gaped. Then, sheepishly and contritely, he returned without any haste to his own home.

Thus Nassir-Yeddin was able to pay all his debts and buy wood and bread. And never again did he and his wife have to suffer hunger.

PAUL GALDONE's long and successful career as an illustrator has been highlighted by countless picture books. In addition to his own versions of many classic folktales, he finds time to illustrate other books, such as *The Queen Who Couldn't Bake Gingerbread* and *The Cool Ride in the Sky* (both Knopf).

Before he set about illustrating *A Strange Servant*, Paul Galdone studied the dress and the culture of the Moslem regions of Russia, the story's setting.

Paul Galdone divides his time between Rockland County, New York, and his farm in Tunbridge, Vermont.

BLANCHE ROSS (1899-1975), translator of *A Strange Servant*, was born in Czechoslovakia. She never entered school, but was tutored at home and allowed to read the books in her father's library. Proficient in six languages, Blanche Ross served as a translator for the U.S. Armed Forces during World War II.